Contents

What is a pebble?

A pebble is a small piece of rock.

You can find lots of them on a beach.

You can easily pick up a pebble.

You can throw it from one hand to another.

How hard is a pebble?

A pebble is **hard**.

When you tap two pebbles together, they make a sound.

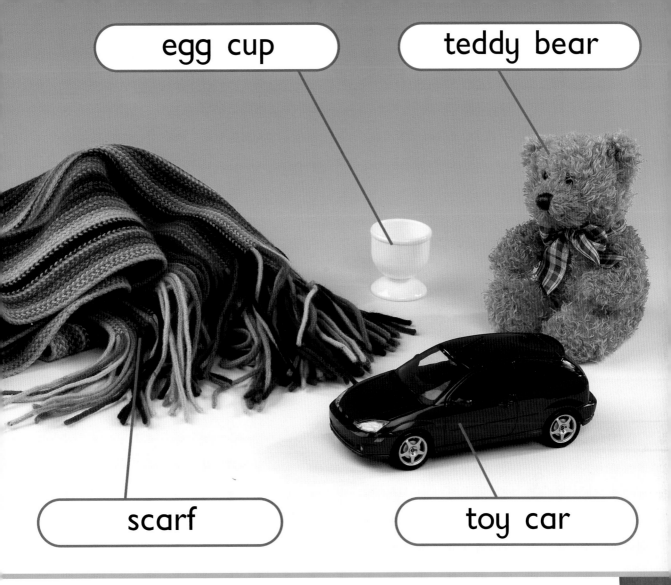

egg cup

teddy bear

scarf

toy car

Which of these things are hard?

Which are soft?

The egg cup and the car are **hard**.

The teddy bear and the scarf feel soft.

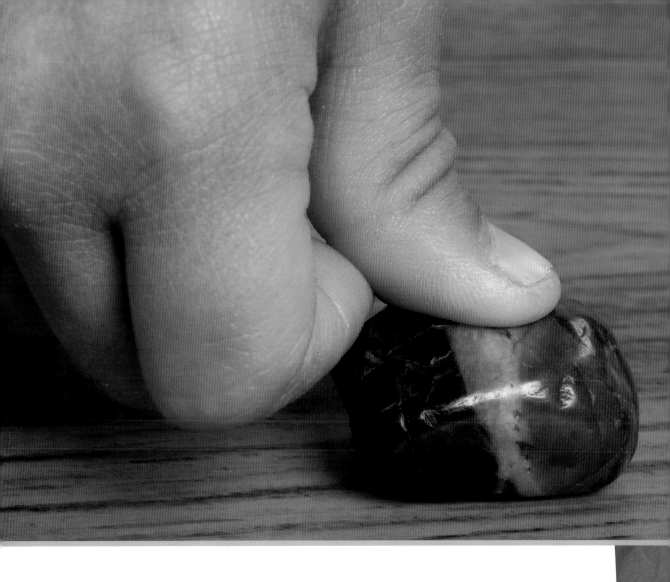

You can **squash** soft things.

You cannot squash a pebble.

Can you scratch a pebble?

You cannot **scratch** a pebble with your fingernail.

The pebble is too **hard**.

Can you scratch a pebble with another pebble?

Yes, you can!

Are pebbles heavy or light?

Pebbles do not feel very heavy because they are small.

socks

ball

apple

teddy bear

pebble

All of these objects are about the same size.

Which one is the heaviest?

The pebble is heavier than each of the other objects.

This large pebble is a **paperweight**.

It is very heavy. It stops the sheets of light paper blowing away.

15

What shape are pebbles?

Pebbles are many different shapes.
Some are round.

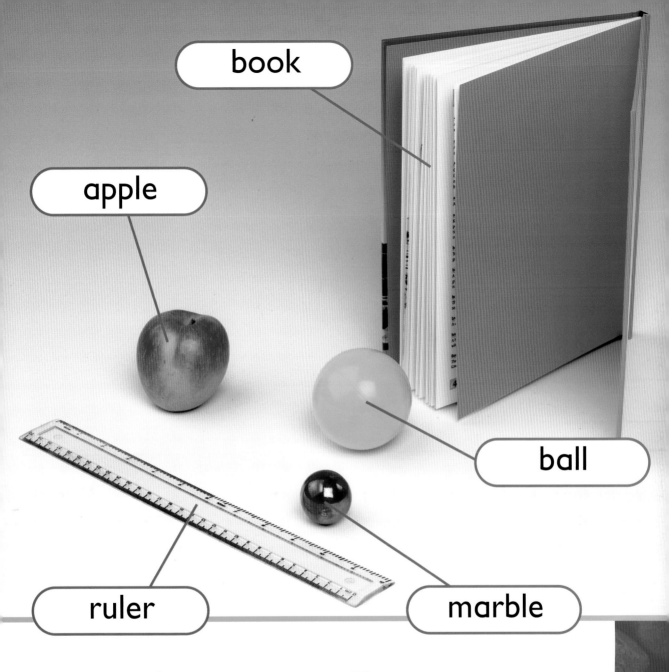

book

apple

ball

ruler

marble

Round objects can **roll**.

Which of these things could you roll?

17

The ball, the marble, and the apple will **roll**.

This round pebble also rolls.

Some pebbles are flat.

Flat objects do not roll.

How are pebbles used?

Pebbles are often used on paths.

They make a **hard** surface for walking on.

Colourful pebbles are used to make **jewellery** and other pretty things.

Quiz

Which of these objects do you think will **roll**?

Look for the answer on page 24.

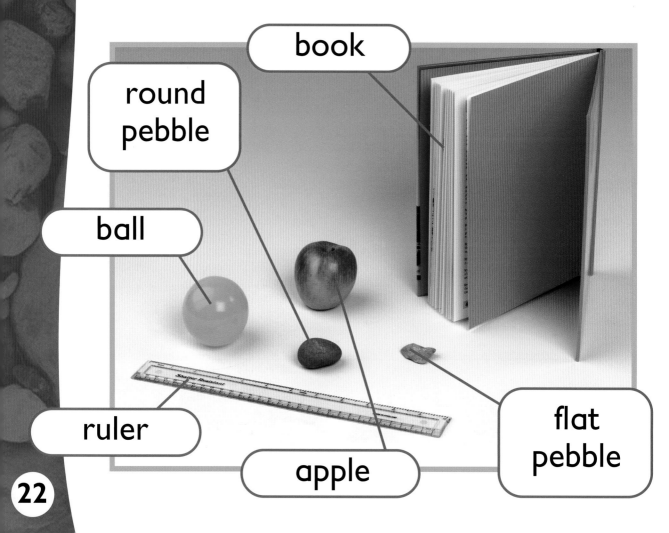

book

round pebble

ball

ruler

apple

flat pebble

Glossary

hard
not soft, so you cannot squash it

jewellery
pretty things that people wear
for decoration

paperweight
heavy object that you put on top of paper
to stop it blowing away

roll
move by turning over and over

scratch
make a mark or small cut

squash
make something flat by pushing it

Index

Answer to quiz on page 22

The round pebble, the ball, and the apple will roll because they are all round.

Note to parents and teachers

Reading for information is an important part of a child's literacy development. Learning begins with a question about something. Help children think of themselves as investigators and researchers by encouraging their questions about the world around them. Each chapter in this book begins with a question. Read the question together. Look at the pictures. Talk about what you think the answer might be. Then read the text to find out if your predictions were correct. Think of other questions you could ask about the topic, and discuss where you might find the answers. Assist children in using the picture glossary and the index to practice new vocabulary and research skills.

Material Detectives: Rock

Let's Look at Pebbles

Angela Royston

www.raintreepublishers.co.uk
Visit our website to find out more information about **Raintree** books.

To order:
☎ Phone 44 (0) 1865 888112
🖹 Send a fax to 44 (0) 1865 314091
💻 Visit the Raintree Bookshop at **www.raintreepublishers.co.uk** to browse our catalogue and order online.

First published in Great Britain by Raintree, Halley Court, Jordan Hill, Oxford OX2 8EJ, part of Harcourt Education.
Raintree is a registered trademark of Harcourt Education Ltd.

Editorial: Andrew Farrow and Sarah Chappelow
Design: Jo Malivoire and AMR
Picture Research: Erica Newbery
Production: Duncan Gilbert

Originated by Modern Age
Printed and bound in China by South China Printing Company

10 digit ISBN 1 844 43634 9 (hardback)
13 digit ISBN 978 1 844 43634 7 (hardback)
10 09 08 07 06
10 9 8 7 6 5 4 3 2 1

10 digit ISBN 1 844 43639 X (paperback)
13 digit ISBN 978 1 844 43639 2 (paperback)
11 10 09 08 07
10 9 8 7 6 5 4 3 2 1

British Library Cataloguing in Publication Data
Royston, Angela
Rock: let's look at pebbles. – (Material Detectives)
620.1'32
A full catalogue record for this book is available from the British Library

Acknowledgements
The publishers would like to thank the following for permission to reproduce photographs:
Gay Bumgarner/Alamy pp. backcover (path) 20; Harcourt Education Ltd p. 21, 23 (jewellery); Peter Johnson/Corbis p. 16; Tudor Photography/Harcourt Education Ltd pp. backcover (apple), 5, 6, 7, 8, 9, 10, 11, 12, 13, 14, 15, 17, 18, 19, 22, 23 (all except jewellery), 24; Zefa/ Masterfile/Mark Tomalty p. 4.

Cover photograph of a pebbly beach reproduced with permission of Hubert Stadler/Corbis.

Every effort has been made to contact copyright holders of any material reproduced in this book. Any omissions will be rectified in subsequent printings if notice is given to the publishers.

The paper used to print this book comes from sustainable resources.

Some words are shown in bold, **like this**. You can find them in the glossary on page 23.